Murder

A comedy-thriller

Bettine Manktelow

Samuel French — London

MURDER WEEKEND

First performed at The Astor Theatre Arts Centre, Deal on
11th-13th September 2003 with the following cast:

Liva Wagstaff	Karen Walker
Sanley Wagstaff	Paul Hilton
Mrs Johnson	Jane Francis
Shelley	Amy Smith
Patsy McAvoy	Sue Thomas
Ashley McAvoy	Richard Sirot
Dorothy Padmore	Christine Bellilli
Violet Jenkins	Pat Hoddinott
Wallace Wainwright	Peter Ryder

Directed by Bettine Walters
Stage Managed by James Murray
Lighting and Sound by Peter Skelton

COPYRIGHT INFORMATION

(See also page ii)

CHARACTERS

Stanley Wagstaff, rather staid business man, conservative in dress and manner; 40s

Livia Wagstaff, Stanley's wife, lively, attractive, restless, looking for adventure; 40s

Mrs Johnson, hotelier, homely, efficient; 40s

Shelley, maid, rather silly; 18

Patsy McAvoy, Livia's friend, insincere, fussy, pretentious and full of envy for Livia; 40s

Ashley McAvoy, Patsy's husband, Livia's lover, attractive, debonair, reckless and unreliable; 40s

Dorothy Padmore, gushing, over-friendly, intent on impressing people with her sincerity; 50s

Violet Jenkins, Dorothy's horsey friend unfriendly, suspicious of others, slightly pompous; 50s

Wallace Wainwright, retired teacher, unassuming and affable; 50s

SYNOPSIS OF SCENES

The action takes place in a country hotel

ACT I
SCENE 1 Hotel reception. Friday afternoon
SCENE 2 The same. Saturday morning

ACT II
SCENE 1 The same. Saturday afternoon
SCENE 2 The same. Saturday evening
SCENE 3 The same. Later that night

Time — the present

AUTHOR'S NOTE

At a "Murder Weekend" guests gather at a hotel or private house to take part in and unravel a murder mystery where they are given secret identities and invited to take part in a fictional plot. It is a game for grown-ups where they are given a certain number of clues to unravel the mystery and the one who does so first wins a prize of some sort.

Bettine Manktelow

Other plays by Bettine Manktelow
published by Samuel French Ltd

Curtain Call
Curtain Up on Murder
Death Walked In
Proscenophobia
They Call It Murder

ACT I

A hotel reception. Friday afternoon

There is an archway LC leading into a hall. There are french windows L leading to the hotel gardens. URC there is a desk/counter with a bell, a registration book and a telephone on it. Above the desk/counter, there is a board with hotel keys attached. There are two chairs and a small table DL, two armchairs and an occasional table DR and a standard lamp

Livia and Stanley enter. Stanley is carrying a suitcase. Livia is carrying a vanity case

Livia Well, here we are ——
Stanley It looks like it. Nobody to greet us.
Livia I'll ring the bell.

She moves to the desk and rings the bell

Stanley (*irritably*) I hope this is going to work out, Livia. It wasn't my idea.
Livia It wasn't my idea either — not really.
Stanley I would much rather have spent a quiet weekend at home. (*He throws himself discontentedly into a chair DL*) I've been so busy this week, the last thing I want to do is gallivant off just when I really could do with a rest.
Livia Really, you are ungrateful! I thought it was so kind of your mother to send us the booking as a present for our anniversary. She knows we both love detective stories. It was a kind thought!
Stanley What? Sending us on a murder weekend? Do you think she's trying to tell us something?
Livia It *could* be fun.
Stanley That's all very well, but I have a long report to read and digest before Monday's meeting. You know I have. I must sit down and read it before I do anything else.
Livia (*bored*) Tell me about it. (*She sits in an armchair DR*)
Stanley I wish you wouldn't talk in stupid clichés. You watch far too much television.
Livia I suppose I do.

Stanley I don't know why you don't get on with your writing. You gave up your job to get on with your writing and now you hardly do any.

Livia I've got writer's block.

Stanley Well — get it unblocked.

Livia I don't seem to have anything to write about. I've used up my inspiration I suppose.

Stanley Isn't writing supposed to be ten percent inspiration and ninety percent perspiration?

Livia I think that's the definition of a genius and writing a few stories for women's mags doesn't exactly qualify.

Stanley They were quite good little stories, I thought — as far as they went.

Livia What do you mean — as far as they went?

Stanley Well — they weren't exactly profound.

Livia Of course they weren't. They weren't meant to be. They were just entertainments. Even Graham Greene claimed that some of his novels were merely entertainments.

Stanley I hope you're not comparing yourself to Graham Greene.

Livia I'm not comparing myself to anyone, but you don't have to be so patronizing, do you? Perhaps my stories weren't much but I made a few pounds and it was nice to see my name in print.

Stanley Then persevere — why don't you?

Livia I've tried. I just haven't any ideas.

Stanley Perhaps this weekend will give you some ideas. Then at least it won't be a complete waste of time. I certainly didn't want to come. You arranged it all behind my back.

Mrs Johnson enters quietly and stands behind the desk

Livia and Stanley are unaware of her

Livia It was meant to be a little surprise. You don't tell people about a surprise, do you?

Stanley It was a surprise too far as far as I'm concerned!

Mrs Johnson coughs politely

Stanley Oh — good-evening.

Mrs Johnson May I help you?

Stanley Oh yes, we'd like to register. Mr and Mrs Wagstaff. (*He crosses to the desk*)

Mrs Johnson Oh yes, of course, Mr and Mrs Wagstaff. For the murder weekend.

Livia That's right.

Mrs Johnson opens the registration book

Mrs Johnson If you would just enter your name and address. You're the first to arrive. I expect two other couples this evening and one tomorrow. That will be our full complement. Eight is quite enough.

Stanley begins to write in the book

Livia Only eight!
Mrs Johnson Eight is just right for a murder weekend. We don't want too many suspects do we?

Shelley enters behind the counter

Shelley *(as she enters)* Mrs Johnson, could you come quickly. There's a problem in the kitchen …
Mrs Johnson Very well, dear. *(To Stanley)* Please excuse me.

Shelley and Mrs Johnson exit

Livia rises and crosses L to the french windows

Livia It really is quite pleasant. I wonder who else will be here.
Stanley *(gloomily)* What does it matter?
Livia There's quite a large garden with fruit trees. It's all laid out — you know, landscaped. I shall have a stroll round there later on.
Stanley Yes, go on, enjoy it. I haven't time to stroll around.
Livia Do try to be nice!
Stanley I will — once I have got that report off my mind. I promise I will try.
Livia That's something. What is the report?
Stanley Waste disposal — I told you.
Livia *(with a yawn)* Oh yes — I believe you did. *(She sits DL by the table)*
Stanley I know it's not glamorous but it *is* important — vitally important actually to the future of the country, to the future of the world in fact.
Livia I hate it when you get earnest.
Stanley I hate it when you don't understand how important my work is.
Livia I do understand. It's just so boring talking about it.
Stanley I thought your women's magazines advise you to encourage a man to talk about his work.
Livia Oh yes, a *man* when you're getting to know him. But not your *husband*. That's different.
Stanley Sometimes the things you say are just — so shallow!

Livia I'm sorry. I know I'm flippant. If I try to be serious I want to cry.

Stanley That is equally ridiculous! You really should pull yourself together.

Livia That's what the psychiatrist said to the patient who told him he felt like a pair of curtains. "Pull yourself together, man!"

Stanley There you go again, just facetious and — and downright silly at times.

Livia I repent! I promise you I will be good!

Stanley I'll believe that when it happens! I do wish someone would show us to our room. I could unpack and have a look at my report and get it out of the way. (*He looks at the registration book*) I think I'll find the room for myself then I can go up and start reading that report. Let's see ... Number nineteen ...

Stanley goes behind the desk and makes to take a key off the board

Patsy McAvoy enters. She goes straight to the desk without looking at Livia

Patsy (*to Stanley*) Oh, hallo — we called to book for the murder weekend. Mr and Mrs McAvoy.

Stanley I'm not ...

Livia (*with a gasp of recognition*) Patsy Greenwalsh!

Patsy What?

Livia Patsy! Patsy Greenwalsh! It's been years, but you haven't changed ... Well, not much — no more than I have.

Patsy (*looking blank*) I'm sorry!

Livia Livia Wagstaff — used to be Webb.

Patsy (*going* DS) Heavens, yes, Livia Webb! I remember you from school. What's your name now, did you say?

Livia Wagstaff.

Patsy Oh, change the name and not the letter, change for worse and not for better! That's what they say. I hope it's not true.

Livia How did you guess!

Patsy What?

Livia Only joking!

Patsy Gosh, the same old Livy! Well, fancy meeting you after all this time. It seems like years ago!

Livia It *was* years ago.

Patsy How strange — what a coincidence — I can't get over it! We *must* talk. What has happened to you?

Livia Oh, just got older — like everyone else.

Ashley enters

Ashley I parked the car. Have you registered?

Patsy Not yet. Just look, darling, an old friend from my school days!

Ashley and Livia look at one another with surprise. Livia looks quickly away

Ashley Oh — how jolly!

Patsy (*with great pride*) My husband, Ashley! You haven't met, have you? Some of the old girls came to my wedding but I don't think you were one of them.

Livia No, I wasn't. We rather drifted apart, didn't we, after school. I haven't had the pleasure of meeting your husband before. I'm Livia Wagstaff, Patsy and I are old school chums.

Ashley Patsy? Oh yes! Well, how do you do. (*Rather too heartily*) What a — pleasant surprise! Meeting an old school chum of my wife! Well!

Livia Yes, quite a surprise!

Patsy What happened to you after you left school, Livia? I always thought you'd do something extraordinary.

Livia Nothing much. Worked in journalism for a while. Now I let my husband keep me so I can write soppy stories for women's mags.

Patsy Oh, how interesting! Ashley writes as well — he's a freelance journalist. Now isn't that a coincidence!

Livia Small world!

Patsy And you write stories? Isn't that fascinating, Ashley? I always read women's magazines in the hairdressers. I wonder if I've read any of your stories?

Livia You wouldn't know if you had. I'm not famous.

Patsy What a shame! But then one never notices the names in magazines, does one? Not unless they are already famous people, I mean. I'm like you. I don't go out to work, either. I'm awfully busy on various charity committees. Besides, Ashley likes me to be at home. I have a young daughter growing up and I have quite enough to do looking after her.

Livia (*with some surprise and with a swift look at Ashley*) A daughter? What a surprise! I mean, how nice!

Patsy You always were creative, Livy. I was just a plodder! We were so different. Strange we were friends. Livia always had a string of boyfriends, Ashley, whereas I married my first. My first and last, I call him. (*She squeezes his arm affectionately*)

Livia How quaint!

Patsy No-one could accuse *you* of being a one-man woman, Livy, as I remember! (*She laughs*)

Stanley coughs self-consciously

Ashley Oh yes — we must book in. (*He hovers by the desk*)

Livia I should have introduced you. This is my husband — Stanley.

Patsy *Your* husband?

Ashley Your *husband*?

Livia This is Patsy Greenwalsh, Stanley. I knew her at school and this is her husband — Ashley.

Patsy Not Greenwalsh — McAvoy.

Livia Of course, I meant McAvoy!

Stan (*to Patsy*) How do you do. (*To Ashley*) How do you do.

Ashley Quite well, thank you. How are you?

Patsy So pleased to meet you! Livia's husband! Sorry, I didn't realize. (*She giggles to hide her embarrassment*) I saw you standing there and I just thought you worked here. You run the hotel between you, I take it? What fun?

Livia No ...

Patsy No?

Stanley No. We're guests as well.

Patsy Oh — but I thought ...

Livia I just went behind the desk to find our key.

Patsy How stupid of me! I'm sorry!

Stanley That's all right.

Patsy What a silly mistake!

Livia That's just like the old Patsy.

Patsy It is?

Stanley Oh, I'm sure it isn't.

Livia How do you know?

Patsy Now I remember — that's so like the old Livia. Speak first and think afterwards! (*She laughs with obvious insincerity*)

Mrs Johnson enters

Mrs Johnson Oh, you must be Mr and Mrs McAvoy. I was expecting you later on. Would you like to register? (*She indicates the registration book*)

Ashley That's the idea! (*He signs in the registration book*)

Mrs Johnson (*looking at Stanley*) Can I help you, Mr Wagstaff?

Stanley I was just looking for our key. We ... That is, I wanted to get unpacked. (*He goes back round the desk*)

Mrs Johnson I'm sorry I was delayed. I'll show you to your room right away.

Livia You take the case up, dear. I was wondering if I might have a cup of tea.

Mrs Johnson Of course — just ring the bell on the desk.

Stanley I'll take the case.

Livia That's what I said.

Mrs Johnson Would you both like to come up? Your room is on the same corridor.

Patsy Yes, please.

Ashley (*looking up from the registration book*; *to Patsy*) I'll be up shortly, dear. I thought I'd like a smoke.

Patsy All right, dear.

Stanley Let me take your case as well.

Patsy How kind!

Stanley No problem!

Patsy See you later, Livia. (*She moves to Mrs Johnson*) It really is the most fantastic coincidence but it turns out that Livia — that is Mrs Wagstaff — and myself are acquainted. We actually went to school together!

Mrs Johnson How extraordinary! What a coincidence!

All three exit via the archway

Left alone, Ashley and Livia look at one another. Livia goes up to ring the bell on the desk. Ashley takes out his cigarettes

Livia Do you really want to smoke? You know I hate it.

Ashley Then I won't. (*He puts them away again*) It was just an excuse to stay down here.

Livia So was mine. What a shock! You turning up here and then being married to Patsy Greenwalsh!

Ashley It was a shock to me as well. I mean meeting you.

Livia I thought I'd never see you again.

Ashley So did I.

Livia What made you come here?

Ashley The booking was sent to us as a result of some facile competition I entered, solving a mystery. I was really surprised to receive tickets. Couldn't even remember entering it for sure, but after all — it was free, so why not accept? I had no idea I was going to meet you!

Livia Obviously not!

Ashley It has been a long time.

Livia Almost a year. (*She moves away from him looking out front*) It was last autumn. I walked away and the leaves were falling off the trees. I cried a bit.

Ashley I *felt* like crying.

Livia It seemed harmless enough in the beginning, didn't it? Two lonely writers meeting up to commiserate over the intransigence of publishers.

Ashley We could have communicated on the net. We didn't have to meet. We have no-one to blame but ourselves.

Livia Do we have to apportion blame? This isn't our fault, is it? We didn't plan to meet now.

Ashley (*going to her*) It must be fate!
Livia Do you really believe that?
Ashley Of course — what else?

They stand looking earnestly into one another's eyes

Shelley enters through the archway

Shelley Did you ring the bell?
Livia (*disconcerted*) Yes please. Tea. What about you, Ashley?
Ashley Tea would be nice.
Livia Tea for two.
Shelley Yes, madam, right away.

Shelley exits

Livia (*reproachfully*) You told me you were separated from your wife.
Ashley I was at the time — but it was only temporary. She was on holiday with her sister.
Livia You lied to me!
Ashley I didn't lie. I just didn't tell all the truth.
Livia You also forgot to mention a daughter. How old is she?
Ashley Twelve.
Livia *Twelve*! You were hardly available, were you?
Ashley Neither were you!
Livia Stanley and I were going through a bad patch. I just felt I needed something to happen in my life. I didn't mean it to turn out the way it did.
Ashley No, I didn't either.
Livia It's such a shock finding you're married to somebody I know.
Ashley I can't help that. We agreed not to mention the past. Our lives began when we met — that's what we said.

Livia crosses in front of Ashley DR

Livia But Patsy Greenwalsh! Of all people! I wouldn't have got involved with you at all if I'd known. It seems disgusting, like sleeping with a relative. I never got on with her at school, you know, not Patsy Greenwalsh!
Ashley I call her Trish.
Livia Trish? A pet name — how sweet!
Ashley That sounded a bit — bitter.
Livia A bit bitter? I suppose it was.
Ashley There's no need to be. (*He crosses to Livia*) I didn't mean to deceive you.

Livia At least I didn't pretend to be separated from my husband.

Ashley Just bored with him! I must say he looks a bit of a stick-in-the-mud.

Livia At least he doesn't tell lies!

Ashley As far as you know!

Livia This is ridiculous! (*She tries to avoid him and crosses in front of him to* L) How are we going to get through the weekend? Perhaps we should book out; Stanley isn't keen on it, anyway. He wouldn't take much persuading.

Ashley There was a time when we would have looked upon this as a bonus, being thrown together for a whole weekend!

Livia Not with our respective spouses in tow.

Ashley (*following Livia*) Can't we still look upon it as an adventure? Make the most of it. Live for today like we used to. To hell with tomorrow!

Livia How fine and reckless!

Ashley You would have thought so once — in the beginning.

Livia I would have thought a lot of things in the beginning. But in the beginning I actually thought it would help my writing. In fact it's had the reverse effect. I haven't written a word for nine months. I've got writer's block. I sit down at the computer and nothing comes. It's like mental constipation.

Ashley How uncomfortable!

Livia It's tragic!

Ashley Perhaps seeing me will unblock it.

Livia That might just make it worthwhile!

Ashley Just seeing you again makes it worthwhile to me.

Livia This gets increasingly like *Brief Encounter*. Any minute I shall expect the train whistle to blow and you will disappear from my life forever! I shall try to keep a stiff upper lip!

Ashley No don't! I can't kiss you if you do!

Livia Do you want to?

Ashley As much as ever.

They look at one another intensely and then fly into each other's arms

Shelley enters with a tea-tray and gives a polite cough

Shelley Your tea, madam.

Livia Thank you — but ... I must have some fresh air.

She rushes out via the french windows

Ashley Oh, dear ...(*He looks at Shelley, nonplussed*) I'd better see what's wrong ...

Ashley exits via the french windows after Livia

Shelley stands holding the tea-tray uncertainly

Mrs Johnson enters behind the desk

Shelley Oh, Mrs Johnson, I got some tea for that lady and then she rushed off into the garden. Shall I leave it in case she comes back?
Mrs Johnson Yes, all right, dear, but be sure to put it on her bill.
Shelley I don't know who she is.
Mrs Johnson It must have been Mrs Wagstaff.
Shelley Her husband dashed after her. I don't know what they're playing at.
Mrs Johnson That wasn't her husband. I'd just shown him to their room.
Shelley Well, I thought it was. When I came in ——
Mrs Johnson (*behind the desk*) Never mind about that. Put the tray down, dear. You look so silly standing there nursing it.

Shelley puts the tray down on the table DL

Now, I must sort out the bookings. There are two ladies to come tonight and one more couple tomorrow — I've got their identities worked out. Where are the envelopes? I'd like you to pass them out in the morning.
Shelley They're all ready.
Mrs Johnson That's good. Now stop moping about and cheer yourself up. There's a lot to do before tomorrow.

Shelley begins to go towards the exit, then stops

Shelley Mrs Johnson, have you thought any more about what I asked you?
Mrs Johnson About living-in? Well, I don't know. It's awkward.
Shelley It's just that I can't stand it at home much longer. My new stepmother is lording it over me like I was a kid! She even had the nerve to tell me not to smoke! And then she backs Dad up when he wants to know where I'm going. I mean, what's it got to do with her?
Mrs Johnson It's always difficult with step-children.
Shelley She actually told me I should call her Mum — and her only ten years older than me! How could she be my mum?
Mrs Johnson It *is* difficult. Well, I don't mind you living-in, dear, but we haven't got much room when we're fully booked. That's why I don't have living-in staff. I need all the rooms to let. Still I'll see if I can find something if it's that bad, but I don't want any problems with your father.
Shelley How could there be problems? You can leave home when you're sixteen now and I'm more than that.

Mrs Johnson Yes, but I know him. I know Jack myself and I don't want any ill feeling.

Shelley I'll say it was my idea, not yours, and I'll tell him why.

Mrs Johnson Perhaps that would be best. It's always best to be honest, that's what I always say. Run along now, dear. Make sure everything is organized for tomorrow.

Shelley Yes, all right.

Shelley exits through the archway. Stanley enters carrying his report

Stanley Oh — is there somewhere I can sit down here to read my report? The bedroom is not somehow conducive to concentration.

Mrs Johnson You'll be all right in here I should think.

Stanley I thought my wife — and —er — Mr What's-'is-name were down here.

Mrs Johnson They went into the garden. They haven't touched their tea, if you would care for a cup?

Stanley Oh, yes, that's good! I'll settle down here. (*He sits* DL *at the table*)

Mrs Johnson I'll let you have some peace and quiet!

Stanley Thank you!

Stanley pours himself a cup of tea and settles down to read his report with a satisfied sigh

Patsy enters through the archway

Patsy Oh, I thought Ashley was here.

Stanley (*with a sigh*) Your husband? No, apparently he went into the garden with Livia.

Patsy He might have said. (*She peers out of the french windows*) I can't see them.

Stanley It's a big garden.

Patsy Yes.

Pastsy sits down at the table, much to Stanley's annoyance

Is there some tea?

Stanley Help yourself! (*He continues to glance covertly at his report during the following dialogue*)

Patsy What do you think about this, Stanley? You don't mind me calling you Stanley, do you?

Stanley It's my name!

Patsy Of course. What do you think about us meeting up like this? It's so strange meeting Livia again after all this time. I'm sure I'm not at all the sort of friend you'd expect Livia to have had at school.

Stanley I can't say I've ever given much thought to what sort of friends she had at school.

Patsy We're so different. I was a bit of a swot. My parents were very keen for me to excel, although I never actually made much use of my education, getting married so young, and to Ashley — who's never been exactly steady. Fortunately for him or rather us — my father left me quite well off.

Stanley Mm — yes.

Patsy Livia was so different. So popular! She never bothered much with schoolwork but she was good at games. Whereas I was not at all good at games, except for netball. I was really quite good at netball. I wasn't in the school team, though, nothing like that. Not like Livia. I'm sorry. I am chattering on. I don't want to bore you.

Stanley No, it's all right. (*He puts down his report with a sigh*) What were you saying?

Patsy Just about Livia and me. Livia is looking very well, isn't she? You'd never guess her age. I can say that as we're both the same age. You can't deceive someone you went to school with. You should have known Livia in those days, always in and out of scrapes but somehow getting away with it. She left without any qualifications to speak of, yet she seems to have got by. She has a nice husband anyway, if I may say so! In a good job, I expect, and with a nice home. Why, some of those old fuddy-duddies, our teachers, used to predict a bad end for her. In fact my own parents predicted a bad end for her. My father banned me from seeing her at one time.

Stanley Banned you — why ever did he do that?

Patsy Oh, he said she was a bad influence. "A bad lot" was what he said. I think it was because I spoke of her with so much admiration. "You don't want to go down that road, my girl," he said to me.

Stanley What road was that?

Patsy The wrong road, I suppose.

Livia hurries in via the french windows and moves C

Livia Oh, *you're* here.

Stanley As observant as ever, darling.

Livia And Patsy. How nice! I suddenly felt like some tea.

Stanley I'm afraid we've drunk it.

Livia Oh, it doesn't matter. I just took a stroll round the garden. A breath of fresh air. I'm beginning to relax.

Stanley I'm glad someone is.

Patsy Have you seen Ashley?

Livia Yes ... Oh, no, not to speak to. He's having a smoke in the garden. I saw him in the distance.

Patsy That's just like him to go out in the garden to smoke. He always respects other people's feelings. I'll go and look for him. (*She finishes her tea first*) See you later!

Patsy goes out via the french windows

There is a pause

Livia Still grappling with your report?
Stanley Trying to! (*He picks it up and glances at it as they talk*) There isn't a comfortable chair in the bedroom.
Livia At least it's quiet down here.
Stanley It must have been quieter in the garden. Why did you come in?
Livia Oh, I just felt like a cup of tea.
Stanley Then why did you go out? Really, Livia, you take some understanding sometimes.
Livia Then don't try!
Stanley There's no need to snap! If anyone should snap I should. All I want is some peace and quiet. I've had to put up with your old school friend rabbiting on about netball and what you were like at school, as if I'm interested, while I'm still grappling with this report.
Livia Sorry, darling. I'll be as quiet as a little mouse! (*She sits in the chair vacated by Patsy*)
Stanley Humph! (*He takes up his report*)

Livia sits quietly for a moment

Livia So, you've been having a nice heart-to-heart, have you? Oh, sorry!
Stanley (*sighing*) *She* was having a heart-to-heart — I didn't encourage her.
Livia I don't suppose she said anything good about me.
Stanley Not much, no.
Livia The feeling was mutual. All I remember about her was that she was boring, spotty and overweight; *always* in tears. She suffered badly from pre-menstrual tension at a certain age. You know what I mean.
Stanley Don't all adolescent girls suffer from something like that? Growing pains and painful crushes on unlikely boys.
Livia You seem to forget it was an all girls' school. The thing we most suffered from was desperate sexual curiosity.
Stanley I imagine *you* soon assuaged that!
Livia We were *all* quite keen to lose our virginity, darling. It was just finding a likely candidate that was difficult.
Stanley Until Ashley came along.
Livia What?

Stanley For Patsy I mean. Ashley — what a poncy name! I don't know why men can't be called Tom, Dick or Harry. You know where you are with a name like that.

Livia Ashley's mother was a great fan of *Gone with the Wind*. It would have been worse if she'd called him Rhett.

Stanley How did you know that?

Livia Know what?

Stanley That Ashley's mother was a fan of *Gone with the Wind*?

Livia I didn't — it was just a joke!

Stanley Oh!

Violet Jenkins (Vi) and Dorothy Padmore (Dotty) enter through the archway. They are both middle-aged women and are dressed in good clothes that don't suit them. Dotty is bouncy and silly and Vi is more reserved but rather abrasive. They both carry suitcases which they leave by the archway before moving into the room

Dotty Oh, hallo!

Stanley Hi ... (*He stands up to greet them*)

Livia Hallo ...

Vi Hallo ...

Dotty Hallo ...

Vi Is there anyone about? We've come for the murder weekend? Have you?

Stanley That's right!

Dotty Oh, it will be fun! I'm so looking forward to it! I'm Dorothy Padmore and this is my friend, Violet Jenkins ...

They all shake hands and exchange greetings

Dotty Everyone calls me Dotty — that's because I am a bit. (*She giggles*)

Vi Don't advertise the fact!

Stanley Stanley Wagstaff — my wife, Livia. (*He quite gives up on his report*)

Dotty Have you come far?

Stanley Up from the coast.

Dotty We've driven from London today — the M25 and M20 — then the scenic route. Quite a good journey once we got off the motorways. I don't care to drive in heavy traffic. I usually leave it to Vi. She swears all the time but she is still much calmer than me. I go to pieces! This is quite a nice place, isn't it? What made you think of coming?

Livia It was a present. Coming here for a murder weekend.

Dotty What a lovely idea. Don't you think so, Vi?

Vi What?

Dotty To have a present of a murder weekend. A really lovely idea. Now, us — we're devotees of murder mysteries. We just love them. We've been to ever so many weekends, haven't we, Vi?

Vi Yes — a few.

Dotty Quite a few! Of course you mustn't tell people about your identity, nothing like that. That would spoil it.

Livia How many have you been on?

Dotty Oh, ever so many, whenever we can get away. We run a nursing home, you see, between us. We don't have much spare time. The beauty and the beast they call us, but I won't say which is which! (*She laughs pleasantly*)

Stanley Isn't that rather unkind — to one of you?

Dotty Oh no, Vi doesn't mind!

Mrs Johnson enters behind the desk

Mrs Johnson Good-afternoon — you must be ...

Dotty Mrs Jenkins and Mrs Padmore.

Mrs Johnson That's right. Would you like to sign in? I have a nice twin-bedded room for you, overlooking the garden. (*She finds their key on the board*)

Dotty Oh, thank you, darling. You are kind! (*She signs in the registration book*) I was just saying we had quite a nice journey down considering we had to use the M25!

Mrs Johnson That's good! You've met Mr and Mrs Wagstaff?

Dotty Yes, we have! We were just discussing murder weekends. We've been to ever so many.

Mrs Johnson Are you experts?

Dotty Oh, no, I wouldn't say that. But we do enjoy a good solution. The last one we went on, the victim was murdered in the bath. That was quite a puzzle, because the door was locked on the inside.

Stanley I hope the solution was plausible.

Dotty Oh yes — the murderer supposedly climbed out of the window. Vi worked that one out.

Vi It was simple. It reminded me of the brides in the bath murders George Joseph Smith. Hanged at Maidstone jail 1915 but that was after he'd seen off three brides. Did it for their money. Quite nifty. Waited till the woman was in the bath and pulled up her heels holding her head under!

Dotty He didn't have to escape through the window, though, did he? He was simply in the room next door. He always did it on their honeymoon in a hotel. But when you think about it they must have splashed about a lot and he would have been soaked and so would the floor. It's amazing nobody noticed.

Vi Water is much easier to clear up than blood!

Dotty Yes, darling, of course but when someone drowns doesn't blood come out of their mouths? You remember when we saw that film about Houdini? He was held upside down in a huge container full of water and blood came out of his mouth.

Vi Perhaps his lungs burst.

Dotty Yes, darling, something like that.

Stanley In actual fact he didn't die like that at all.

Dotty Who?

Stanley Houdini. He had a ruptured appendix. He said he had cast-iron muscles and invited someone to hit him in the stomach but unfortunately they did it when he wasn't prepared and it ruptured his appendix.

Dotty Golly — how did you know that?

Stanley One of my hobbies, knowing things like that.

Livia (*sarcastically*) Never know when that kind of information might come in handy.

Vi No knowledge is wasted. Especially when you're trying to solve a murder mystery. Store it away — that's what I say.

Dotty That's Vi all over. She's a mine of information about murder and violent death, aren't you, Vi?

Vi (*with modest pride*) Not bad.

Mrs Johnson Shall I show you to your room? (*She comes round from behind the desk*)

Dotty Oh yes, please — Vi will get the cases, won't you, dear?

Vi OK ... (*She picks up the cases by the archway*)

Dotty We'll see you later then? At dinner. Won't it be fun?

Stanley Yes — I look forward to it.

Mrs Johnson moves towards the exit with Dotty and Vi, Dotty still talking as she goes

Dotty I think this must be about our tenth murder mystery weekend ...

They exit

Stanley picks up his report with an irritated gesture and sits DR *in an armchair*

Stanley My God, what have we let ourselves in for!

Livia The beauty and the beast! What an odd couple!

Ashley enters via the french windows

Ashley Oh, here you are!

Stanley (*crossly*) Yes, here we are! Your wife went to look for you.
Ashley I saw her — only I missed her.
Stanley How did you do that?

*During the following, Ashley and Livia look dreamily at one another clearly
not thinking about what they are saying*

Livia It's such a large garden.
Ashley Mm, yes. So much to see.
Livia You can smell the mimosa. Did you notice?
Ashley Ah yes — the mimosa! Very pleasant — the mimosa!
Livia That's what I think! Very pleasant!
Stanley (*rising with a sigh*) I'll just go upstairs to read this. I've read the same
    bloody sentence ten times already and it still hasn't sunk in.
Livia Sorry, darling! Were we distracting you?
Stanley (*wearily*) Not at all!

Stanley exits

Livia and Ashley look at one another and then dash into one another's arms

Livia What are we doing?
Ashley What are we going to do?
Livia I don't know! I don't care!

They embrace again

Ashley This is awful! I still feel the same! I just didn't realize how much I
    missed you.
Livia Neither did I!
Ashley It was madness, wasn't it?
Livia Those rapturous afternoons in an anonymous motel ...
Ashley The long days in between ...
Livia The re-unions!
Ashley Darling!
Livia Darling!

They embrace again

*Wallace Wainwright enters. He is a tall man wearing a caped overcoat and
a deerstalker hat*

Wallace Good-evening! Have you a room for the night?

Livia gives a little shriek and backs away

Ashley Oh my God! Sherlock Holmes!

Black-out

CURTAIN

SCENE 2

The same. Saturday morning

As the Lights come up Mrs Johnson is talking on the telephone

Patsy enters via the french windows

Mrs Johnson (*into the telephone*) You will keep me posted, Jack, won't you? I can't help being a bit worried. ... Yes, all right, I'll try! Cheerio! (*She hangs up*)
Patsy What a lovely morning! I've just been admiring your rhododendrons.
Mrs Johnson We do try to keep things pretty.
Patsy And please compliment the chef on the breakfast. It was delicious. Particularly the black pudding. You hardly ever have a good black pudding South of Watford.
Mrs Johnson I shall tell chef. It was a bit of a problem this morning because the girl didn't turn up. You know Shelley.
Patsy Oh yes — the pretty girl, Shelley. She didn't turn up today! I wonder why! Perhaps she's ill.
Mrs Johnson I rang her home but they haven't seen her since last night. It is a nuisance.
Patsy Aren't they worried?
Mrs Johnson No — apparently, they're used to it.
Patsy Young people today! When I was young — oh, I couldn't even imagine what would have happened to me if I'd stayed out all night without telling my parents first. They wouldn't have allowed me even then.
Mrs Johnson Times change!
Patsy They certainly do.
Mrs Johnson You have your identity, haven't you? It was in an envelope on the breakfast table.
Patsy (*producing a white envelope*) Oh yes, thank you! I haven't actually opened it yet! Keeping it a secret from Ashley.
Mrs Johnson Oh yes, that's most important. Entering into the spirit of things. Well, I must get on.

Mrs Johnson exits

Vi and Dotty enter through the archway. They are dressed for going out

Dotty Oh, hallo!
Patsy Good-morning. I was just saying what a good breakfast it was. I love black pudding.
Dotty So do I!
Vi Pig's blood!
Patsy What?
Vi Black pudding is pig's blood.
Patsy Oh dear, it doesn't sound nice, does it?
Dotty But it tastes nice! That's just like you, Vi, to say something like that. (*To Patsy*) I see you've got your identity.
Patsy What? Oh yes, I have. I haven't opened it yet.
Dotty We have. I couldn't wait. You know you mustn't say who you are.
Patsy Of course not.
Dotty We don't even tell one another, do we, Vi?
Vi Certainly not! That would spoil the fun.
Patsy It must be nice to have a real friend to go around with.
Dotty Oh it is!
Patsy Don't your husbands mind you coming away without them?
Vi Husbands! We ditched them long ago.
Dotty I should say so! No man could compare with Vi for companionship.
Vi Ditto.
Patsy (*a little nonplussed*) Well, how nice!

Wallace enters via the french windows. He is minus his caped coat and deerstalker hat

Patsy Oh — hallo, you arrived last night, didn't you?
Wallace Wallace Wainwright.
Patsy I'm Patricia McAvoy and these ladies are ... Oh, I'm sorry I've forgotten your names.
Dotty Mrs Padmore ... (*Simpering*) Call me Dotty.
Vi Violent Jenkins. (*She nods curtly*)
Wallace Lovely day, isn't it, ladies?

Wallace shakes hands with Dotty and then crosses R

I just saw a squirrel outside — grey one of course, but nonetheless very decorative — ran across my path as bold as anything. Wonderful, isn't it, to be in the country?
Patsy Oh yes, wonderful! My husband said when you arrived last night he thought you were Sherlock Holmes.

Wallace It wasn't intentional. I picked up the coat in Oxfam and the hat I've
had for years. Of course when he explained it was a murder weekend I
could see the funny side.

Patsy Didn't you come here for the murder weekend?

Wallace Not at all. My car broke down on the bypass. I was towed to the
nearest garage but they told me they couldn't get the spare part until
Monday, so here I am, stuck! Fortunately they found room for me here.

Patsy We quite thought we were going to have to dress up when we heard
about you coming as Sherlock Holmes!

Vi Did that once. Won't do it again. Felt bloody silly!

Dotty Poor Vi, they made her dress as a maid!

Vi Dreadful! Never wear frocks! Hate the things.

Patsy Yes, I don't think I'd want to dress up unless it was something
glamorous! Different from myself, that is! (*With a forced laugh*) Oh —
there's my husband! Everybody is taking a stroll in the garden this
morning. Yoohoo! He's with my old school chum, Livia. Strange isn't it?
We should meet up again here. We haven't seen each other for — oh, it
must be twenty years. Here they come.

*Ashley and Livia enter via the french windows. Livia looks slightly
dishevelled and has grass seeds attached to her back*

Have you had a nice stroll?

Ashley Drove the cobwebs away.

*Ashley remains standing by Patsy. Livia moves across stage in front of Dotty
and Vi*

Livia It was nice.

Patsy I didn't see you. Where were you?

Livia }(*together*){ There's a meadow …
Ashley }   { There's a field …

Dotty You sound as if you're going to burst into song! (*She giggles*)

Vi They could harmonize!

Dotty and Vi both laugh

Ashley I just happened to climb a stile over there to go into the field and ran
into Livia coming back.

Livia Yes, I was coming back.

Dotty Well, you must have fallen over. You've got grass seeds all over your
back.

Livia Oh — have I? Oh yes, I did, I fell over backwards when I was climbing
the stile.

Patsy Oh dear, did you hurt yourself?

Livia No, no, not really.

Ashley I caught her.

Dotty If you'd caught her she wouldn't have got grass seeds on her back, would she?

Livia No, he didn't actually catch me — helped me up.

Ashley That's right. I helped her up.

Patsy You missed breakfast, Livia.

Livia I never eat breakfast.

Patsy You should. It's the most important meal of the day. Besides you have paid for it.

Vi Doesn't your husband eat breakfast either?

Livia He had a continental in the room. He has an awful report to finish reading, poor darling! It's five hundred pages! Practically a book.

Dotty In connection with his work, is it?

Livia Yes, he's in waste disposal. (*Pause*) Funny! That's always guaranteed to shut people up. (*To Wallace*) You're the man who checked in last night. I hardly recognized you without your hat and coat.

Wallace I don't wear them all the time.

Livia You must have a pipe to match — what are they called — a meerschaum?

Wallace I'd love to have one — but I wouldn't know where to start looking.

Livia And I'll bet you play the violin!

Wallace No, no, I told you. I was not trying to be Sherlock Holmes — I'm the last person, believe me! I'm a retired teacher. I'm not clever at all.

Patsy You're very modest!

Ashley I must say we were impressed last night. I thought it just set the scene for the weekend until you explained what really happened.

Wallace Sorry to disappoint you.

Livia Still, since you're here, you might as well join in.

Wallace I wouldn't be any good at it.

Livia How do you know? You might be.

Wallace I'm on my way to Peterborough to see my daughter. I don't really know what to do, because I must wait for the car. I suppose I'll have to stay for the weekend. (*He wanders upstage between Dotty and Vi*) There's no point in going up by train and coming back here some time next week. No point at all.

Dotty There, you see, you might as well join in. It's all the better to have more people.

Patsy And we haven't started yet. Any of us. All we have is our identities.

Dotty You could ask for an identity, though I suppose they've already picked out the murderer.

Ashley Yes, they must have, but no crime has been committed as yet.

Vi As far as we know.

Dotty Oh, Vi — you sounded so ominous. What do you mean, as far as we know? Do you think it's started without us realizing it?

Vi If I was organizing it I certainly wouldn't wait for a starting pistol to go off!

Patsy I see what you mean. If they started without telling us that would require some real ingenuity to work out.

Vi Exactly!

Patsy So you see, Mr Wainwright, you might be involved without even knowing it!

The telephone rings. They all turn and look at it

Mrs Johnson rushes in and picks up the receiver

Everyone else listens to the conversation

Mrs Johnson (*into the phone*) Yes? Oh, Jack, it's you! Any sign of Shelley yet? I'm in quite a fix. What? ... I don't understand. ... Say again. ... Her bicycle? ... But what does it mean?... Oh dear! I am sorry, Jack ... You've called the police? ... What do they think? ... No, they never say, do they? Oh dear, what a worry for you! ... Yes, of course we must all hope for the best. ... Yes, yes, I understand. ... Just keep in touch. ... Let me know. I'm here if you want me. (*She hangs up*) That was Shelley's father. She didn't go home last night at all and now they've found her bike in a ditch, but there's no sign of *her*!

Patsy Oh, dear, what could have happened to her?

Mrs Johnson They don't know.

Livia Do you mean she's disappeared?

Mrs Johnson It looks like it.

Vi (*tugging at Dotty's arm*) I think it's started.

Dotty Do you, really?

They turn to look at the others accusingly

CURTAIN

ACT II

Scene 1

The same. Saturday afternoon

As the Curtain *rises, Stanley and Livia are sitting* DL *either side of the small table. There is a newspaper on the table*

Livia So anyway, what happened is that the Dotty woman ——
Stanley What dotty woman?
Livia The one called Dotty — *you* know, don't be so obtuse.
Stanley All right — go on!
Livia Well, after her friend blurted out "I think it's started!" that Dotty woman turned and stared at Mrs Johnson accusingly and Mrs Johnson looked daggers at her and walked out!
Stanley So what do you conclude from that?
Livia I don't know, that's why I'm asking you. Did it mean that it had started, or it hadn't started?
Stanley You mean — the murder weekend?
Livia Exactly. Is the disappearance of this girl part of the weekend that we have to unravel or is it genuine? It's important to know.
Stanley If it isn't part of it we've been cheated.
Livia Why do you say that?
Stanley Because here it is, Saturday afternoon and nothing's happened yet. I mean, when *does* it start?
Livia I thought another couple were expected.
Stanley So did I.
Livia I think we should go home.
Stanley Why, for God's sake? You make me cross! We're here now. It's paid for and whether we have to take part in some silly game or other doesn't really matter. I've got on top of my report and now I want to relax and just enjoy what's left of the weekend. (*He picks up the paper and hides behind it*)
Livia I think it would be better if we went home. It isn't working out.

She waits for Stanley to comment but he doesn't

I'm not happy about running into Patsy either. I never got on with her at school.

Stanley rustles the newspaper but does not surface

Are you listening to me?
Stanley Not if I can help it.
Livia You're infuriating! I'm going for a walk.
Stanley Good! Enjoy it!

Livia gives him a derisory glance and exits via the french windows

Mrs Johnson comes in through the   archway

Mrs Johnson Oh, are you all right, Mr Wagstaff? Anything you want?
Stanley (*looking over the top of his newspaper*) Wouldn't mind a cup of tea.
Mrs Johnson I'll see to it. Tea for two?
Stanley No — just one. My wife has gone for a walk.

Mrs Johnson turns to go

No news, I suppose, about the girl?
Mrs Johnson Not since this morning. Quite worrying, isn't it?
Stanley There's probably some perfectly simple explanation.
Mrs Johnson I can't help thinking of the times I've read in the newspaper
   about an abandoned bike being found in a ditch somewhere and it always
   seemed to signify something sinister had happened.
Stanley Not always — people are always abandoning their bikes, worn-out
   rusty old things all over the place.
Mrs Johnson Yes, but not when they are on their way home in a quiet
   country lane, and when the bike was perfectly serviceable. There was
   nothing wrong with it, the police said, not even a puncture. I mean she
   might have abandoned it if she'd had a puncture, but even so she would
   have walked home or come back here. Not just disappeared.
Stanley Perhaps she's taken off with some boyfriend, gone to Gretna Green
   or something like that!
Mrs Johnson She isn't the type to go off somewhere, not Shelley.
Stanley I suppose the game is still on? The murder weekend?
Mrs Johnson Of course. Running a hotel is like show business. The show
   must go on! You mustn't disappoint the public.
Stanley Only there doesn't seem to be all the guests you were expecting.
Mrs Johnson Two cancelled this morning. No explanation! Very
   inconsiderate. They'll lose their deposit of course.
Stanley So we are rather a small band of suspects, after all.
Mrs Johnson Ah, those little grey cells will have to work even harder!

Stanley disappears behind his newspaper once more

Patsy enters through the archway. She is absurdly bright, covering up some secret anxiety

Patsy Oh — Mrs Johnson — sorry to bother you but have you seen my husband?
Mrs Johnson I'm sorry, no.
Patsy He keeps disappearing. It's quite a small hotel and yet whenever I look round he's not there.

Stanley rustles his paper but says nothing

Patsy I think we were wondering if the murder weekend is still on.
Mrs Johnson Of course it is. I've just been assuring Mr Wagstaff of that fact. The show must go on!
Patsy Oh, well, I'm sure we will all enjoy the weekend whether there's a murder or not! That does sound funny, doesn't it? I mean anyone overhearing who didn't know what we were talking about, they'd think it was odd saying we can enjoy it whether there's a murder or not!
Mrs Johnson We've advertised it and we must fulfil our obligations. Would you like some tea? I was getting some for Mr Wagstaff.
Patsy Yes, thank you. That would be nice!

Mrs Johnson exits

Patsy I'm glad she's left us alone. I wanted to speak to you.
Stanley (*from behind his newspaper*) Anything special?

Patsy sits DL *opposite Stanley*

Patsy It is rather.
Stanley (*putting down his newspaper with a resigned sigh*) Yes?
Patsy What do you think of this? It was left by my plate at breakfast, along with my identity. (*She hands him a folded slip of paper*)
Stanley What identity?
Patsy We all had our identity this morning. You must have seen it, a plain white envelope left by everyone's plate.
Stanley *I* didn't have one.
Patsy You must have done. I had two envelopes. One was my identity and then this one — they were both typed. Just read it.

Stanley reads the slip of paper. He hands it back to Patsy, rises and moves across to sit in an armchair DR. *He is disturbed by what he has read*

Stanley I don't believe it. Livia would have told me. She isn't like that.
Patsy She used to be.
Stanley You're talking about when she was a silly teenager. She isn't like
that now. What does your husband say?
Patsy I haven't asked him. I wanted to know what you thought first.
Stanley It's rubbish! If I were you I'd just ignore it.
Patsy It's so puzzling. It looks like the same paper and the same typing. You
don't think Mrs Johnson would go to these lengths for her murder mystery,
surely?
Stanley Of course not! It must be a joke — but it's in very poor taste.
Patsy I do hope you're right.

Wallace enters via the french windows

Wallace I've just seen a police car coming up the drive. I wonder if it's
significant.
Patsy Oh — about the girl!
Wallace Could be!
Patsy I hope it's not bad news.
Wallace Who knows?
Patsy Do you think it could be part of the game? The murder weekend.
Wallace I hardly think they'd go as far as to involve the police, would they?
Just for a game? Wouldn't that be considered wasting police time?
Patsy I suppose it would. But if they found out something has happened to
her — we'll all have to be questioned, won't we?
Wallace I don't see why. (*He crosses to* R) After all, none of us *know*
anything, do we?
Stanley What is there to know?
Wallace Exactly! What is there to know?

Dotty and Vi enter through the archway

Dotty (*excitedly*) The police are at the door.
Wallace Yes, we know.
Dotty They showed Mrs Johnson something. I don't know what it was.
Vi A garment of some description.
Patsy Oh dear, that sounds ominous!
Vi I didn't see any blood — but we were not very close.
Dotty There might not have been any blood. It could have been ripped off
and thrown away into the bushes before — anything else happened to her.
Stanley Or she could simply have discarded it. It's useless to speculate.
Wallace Of course we mustn't speculate — but you can't help wondering ...

Livia and Ashley enter via the french windows. They are both breathless and look dishevelled

Ashley We saw a police car ...

Livia Does it mean anything?

Stanley Not much. They found a garment and showed it to Mrs Johnson. That's all we know.

Livia A garment!

Patsy Where have you two been this time? You look a bit — messy!

Livia Just walking. I fell over!

Ashley Yes, she fell over.

Stanley You always seem to be falling over these days, darling!

Livia Silly, isn't it? I'm not used to the country. I wear the wrong shoes.

Dotty We saw you just now!

Livia (*nervously*) Oh, did you? Where?

Vi At the edge of the field. You seemed to emerge from the grass. We couldn't make you out properly.

Dotty What *were* you doing? I thought it was bird watching. You looked so tense — your body looked tense. We couldn't see your face properly. I said to Vi, "Oh, she's birdwatching."

Livia That's right. That's just what I was doing.

Stanley I've never known my wife interested in birdwatching before.

Livia Oh, you're so wrong, darling. (*She sits in the armchair to him* DR) I've been a secret twitcher for years!

Vi What was it?

Livia What was what?

Vi The bird.

Livia Oh, it was a — a ...

Ashley (*coming to her rescue*) It was a — a seldom-seen crested plover.

Vi A seldom-seen what?

Ashley A crested plover.

Vi Never heard of it!

Patsy You saw it, too, did you, Ashley? This bird.

Ashley Ah no, I didn't actually see it. Livia told me ...

Patsy Where were you — when she told you?

Ashley I was — approaching.

Patsy Approaching!

Ashley Mm, yes ... I was approaching across the garden and Livia called out to me, "I think that's a seldom-seen crested plover."

Stanley And what did you say?

Ashley What did I say? Oh — nothing much, just sorry I missed it ... Something like that.

Vi It's strange that if you were in the garden we didn't see you.

Ashley Oh — I was in the — er kitchen garden.
Patsy Where's that?
Ashley (*triumphantly*) Outside the kitchen!
Vi We still would have seen you.
Dotty (*covering up for him*) Oh, we might not, Vi. We can't see round corners, can we?

Mrs Johnson enters behind the desk. She carries two cups of tea on a tray

Mrs Johnson Oh, you're all here. Does anyone else want anything? (*She takes Stanley a cup of tea* DR *and then crosses and takes one to Patsy* DL)
Dotty No — not really, thank you, not for us at any rate.
Mrs Johnson That's all right then ...
Vi We're dying to know what the police wanted, that's all.
Mrs Johnson The police?
Vi We saw them at the door.
Mrs Johnson Oh yes, the police.
Dotty We wondered — what was it about?
Mrs Johnson (*sadly*) It was just — her little apron, Shelley's little apron, they found it. In the bushes. (*She sniffs*) She was wearing it when she left here yesterday.
Vi No blood stains?
Mrs Johnson Oh, no! Nothing like that! But not a sign of *her*. I just wish I'd let her stay last night. She didn't want to go home. Oh dear, I feel so guilty. (*Looking round at them*) Still — you mustn't let it spoil your weekend. Just ring the bell if you want anything.

Mrs Johnson exits through the archway

Dotty (*disappointed*) An apron with no blood stains! I wonder what that means.
Vi Nothing, that's what! I'll go up and change my shoes. I trod in something out there! One of the joys of country life!
Dotty Yes, dear, I want to change as well.

Dotty and Vi exit through the archway, talking as they go

Patsy (*accusingly to Ashley*) Your shoes are muddy too, darling, and your trousers. You look as if you've been rolling in the mud.
Ashley Do I? Well, I haven't.
Patsy Frankly, you look a mess! (*She glares at him*)

Livia takes Stan's tea cup and sits down thoughfully

Stan That was *my* tea!
Livia Was it? Oh, sorry! (*She takes a sip and hands it back*)

There is a pause

Patsy I would like a word with you, Ashley, in private.
Ashley What *now*?
Patsy Unless you want a scene down here.
Ashley Ah — *now*! Of course.

Ashley and Patsy exit through the archway

There is a pause

Wallace Time for me to have a turn round the garden, I believe; smoke my pipe.

Wallace goes out via the french windows

Stanley So, what exactly was going on out there in the field? Are you going to enlighten me?
Livia It wasn't anything.
Stanley It certainly wasn't birdwatching.
Livi No, it wasn't *exactly* birdwatching.
Stanley What was it then?
Livia Oh, we were just talking and that ——
Stanley It's the "that" that worries me.
Livia You're just being absurd!
Stanley Am I? You were in the grass *together* I assume, all that nonsense about approaching from the kitchen garden and you calling out "I've just seen a seldom-seen something-something and all that". Come off it!
Livia What are you suggesting? I mean, we've only just met.
Stanley Have you?
Livia Of course we have — don't be so cryptic!
Stanley Only someone here thinks you've met before.
Livia Who?
Stanley Ashley and yourself. You've met before.
Livia Why should anyone think that?
Stanley Have you met before?
Livia Before when?
Stanley Before now!
Livia Of course not.
Stanley Then why should someone suggest you did?

Livia I've no idea. Oh, for heaven's sake stop glaring at me. I'm not going to confess anything. There isn't anything to confess. I've just met the guy. Don't behave like a stupid old grouch! Loosen up a bit, for god's sake!

Stanley Sure, baby, I'll chill out! There you go again, using slang!

Livia (*explosively*) I'm fed up! This weekend isn't working out at all. I think we should go home!

Stanley All right, let's go home! Go up and pack and I'll pay the bar bill.

Livia I will.

Livia storms out through the archway

Stanley goes across to the desk and rings the bell. Pause. Nobody comes

Patsy enters through the archway in tears

Patsy I just passed Livia. She wouldn't stop and speak to me. She was in a temper.

Stanley *She* was in a temper! Humph! (*He rings the bell again*)

Patsy I'm so upset.

Stanley I think I know why.

Patsy My husband and your wife ... That note!

Stanley I've tackled Livia. She denies it.

Patsy Ashley's the same but if it's not true why did they look so guilty when they came in from the garden? Livia Webb of all people! She was always such a bitch! So competitive. She just likes taking someone away from someone, especially someone like me. Oh hell! I wish I'd never come here. I wish I was still in ignorance of it — whatever it was! (*She sniffs and searches for her handkerchief*)

Stanley Oh, steady on! You are rather jumping to conclusions. Perhaps we both are. That note could just be someone making mischief.

Patsy But why should anyone want to make mischief? Poor Ashley is so susceptible and so attractive! I'm not surprised she got her hooks into him. I wonder when it happened or how far it went! Oh, I don't know what I'm going to do! I can't bear it! I just can't bear it! Livia Webb — of all people! What a bitch!

Stanley Here — wait a minute, you are talking about my wife!

Patsy I don't care! I know her. I know it's true. They're carrying on! I feel it in my heart. (*With dramatic emphasis*) I must get out of here! I'll go for a drive.

Stanley I don't think it's a good idea to drive when you're feeling so upset.

Patsy I drive better when I'm feeling upset!

Patsy storms out via the french windows

Stanley gives a sigh and moves towards the desk in order to ring the bell but doesn't get the chance

   Mrs Johnson enters behind the desk

Mrs Johnson (*a bit frostily*) Yes?
Stanley We want to settle up. The bar bill. We had some drinks last night.
Mrs Johnson Oh, that's not necessary until you leave ...
Stanley We are leaving.
Mrs Johnson What, right now?
Stanley Yes — I've just had an urgent text message to get back.
Mrs Johnson Nothing serious, I hope.
Stanley Only work — that's serious enough.
Mrs Johnson It does seem a shame when it's only just begun ...
Stanley What's begun?
Mrs Johnson The murder weekend. Everything that has happened up till now is all part of it.
Stanley *Everything*?
Mrs Johnson Oh yes, everything. Shelley disappearing and everything. Of course they haven't found the body yet but they will next time.
Stanley Next time?
Mrs Johnson That's the next part of it — that they've found the body, ostensibly. Then you'll know it's all part of the plot.
Stanley But the police really were at the door!
Mrs Johnson My nephew. I asked him to pop in when he was by this way, just driving around. Quite a good touch, wasn't it? Now I've told you. But I haven't given too much away, have I? I didn't want you to leave. You'll have to work out the rest for yourself. The first one to find out the solution has a bottle of champagne tomorrow night before leaving.
Stanley I find all this bewildering. I didn't know it had begun.
Mrs Johnson But you must have known. I left an identity beside every-body's plate this morning at breakfast. Didn't you see it? A note.
Stanley A note?
Mrs Johnson That's it. A white envelope beside your plate. You must have seen it.
Stanley Good Lord, the notes by the plates at breakfast!
Mrs Johnson That's right!
Stanley (*relieved*) Livia picked something up — and of course so did her friend! My God, do you mean to say it was all made up? Everything that's happened up till now? It's all part of the plot? Am I the only one who doesn't know?
Mrs Johnson The others should know — if they read the notes I left them. They should all know their identities and what they were supposed to do.
Stanley Oh dear, I'm afraid Mrs McAvoy took your note very seriously.

Mrs Johnson That's good, isn't it?

Wallace enters via the french windows

Wallace Who has a blue Mercedes?
Stanley I don't know — why?
Wallace Someone driving a blue Mercedes nearly ran me over coming up the drive. I had to jump out of the way pretty smartish.
Mrs Johnson Mr and Mrs McAvoy have a blue Mercedes.
Stanley She did run out of here in a state — it must be her. (*To Mrs Johnson*) I told you she took it very seriously.
Mrs Johnson She's only entering into the spirit of things — playing her part.
Wallace You mean — it's started?
Mrs Johnson Oh, I suppose you wouldn't know. You came late, and I wasn't expecting you, so you don't know the part you're supposed to be playing.
Wallace I didn't expect to have a part. I'm just a bystander.
Mrs Johnson You can't be a bystander at a murder weekend.

Livia enters through archway with her vanity case

Livia I'm packed.
Stanley We don't have to leave, darling. It's all right.
Mrs Johnson You're not leaving after all. That's good!
Livia I thought you wanted us to leave.
Stanley Not now I understand. You're better than I thought, darling, at keeping a secret.
Livia I am?
Stanley Not half! (*He puts his arms round her and kisses her*) Go on then — see if you can convince me. I'll still play the injured husband if that makes it easier for you. You convince me!
Livia Convince you — of what?
Stanley Your innocence!
Livia My innocence — of what?
Stanley Everything, darling! Everything!

Livia is completely nonplussed

Wallace This is getting really intriguing. I can see I shall have to join in.

Ashley enters through the archway

Ashley Does anyone know why my car is stuck at the bottom of the drive with the lights on.
Wallace The blue Mercedes?
Ashley That's the one.

Wallace I think your wife was driving it.

Ashley Well, she isn't driving it now. Nobody is! It's just stuck there. I'd better move it before something comes along and runs into it.

Mrs Johnson comes round in front of the desk

Mrs Johnson Oh dear, I'm not at all sure this is meant to happen.

Ashley and Mrs Johnson go off together through the archway

Stanley This is really quite interesting!

Livia That's hardly the word I'd use.

Stanley You're so determined to keep up the pretence, aren't you, darling? All right, I'll play along with you. Let's join the others.

Stanley puts his arm round Livia and leads her out through the archway

Livia (*as they go*) I really can't make out what you mean!

They exit

Wallace (*once he is alone*) Curiouser and curiouser!

CURTAIN

SCENE 2

The same. Saturday evening

As the CURTAIN *rises, Livia is pacing about the room holding a notebook and pencil. She is murmuring to herself*

Wallace enters via the french windows

Livia "They collapsed in an agony of passion into the long grass ..." No, no, better ... "She surrendered in an agony of passion into the long grass." (*She scribbles in the notebook, then catches sight of Wallace*) Oh—I didn't hear you come in.

Wallace Sorry — I didn't mean to startle you.

Livia It's all right. I was just thinking aloud.

Wallace No more dramas — after this afternoon?

Livia No, I think Patsy is all right now. My husband and *her* husband more or less carried her upstairs. She wasn't hurt, just shaken. She bent the front bumper.

Wallace I'm not surprised. She was driving much too fast when I saw her. She made a dent in the gate-post.

Livia A bit daft, really! (*She looks down at her notebook*)

Wallace I hope I'm not disturbing you.

Livia No, it's all right.

Wallace You're writing something?

Livia It's just an idea for a short story. That's what I do — as a hobby — write short stories for women's magazines. Of course that isn't what I *want* to write.

Wallace So what do you want to write?

Livia The Great British Novel. Doesn't every writer?

Wallace That depends how you define the Great British Novel.

Livia Do *you* write?

Wallace I used to years ago without any real success. I wrote a book once. It's still sitting in my desk drawer.

Livia You must persevere.

Wallace I suppose so. I don't seem to have the urge any more.

Livia I couldn't give up writing. It's so much a part of my life. It isn't just about success, that's a by-product.

Wallace What is it about then?

Livia Oh — much more than that! It's therapy — at least it is as far as I'm concerned.

Wallace Is it the most important thing in your life? Like Van Gogh, painting away his madness.

Livia Oh, I'm not mad!

Wallace I'm not suggesting that. I mean does your writing matter more to you than people?

Livia (*puzzled*) Well, no — it's *about* people, after all. "Only connect", isn't that what E M Forster said?

Wallace Ah yes — connecting! That *is* important, you're right there. For a little while we feel less insular, less of an island, trying to connect with a reader. Of course if there is no connection — if you're not published, it all becomes a bit pointless.

Livia (*not really listening*) I suppose so.

Wallace Though nowadays I suppose you can always link up with other writers. There is an organization, isn't there, for writers to chat with one another?

Livia (*warily*) I don't know. I believe so.

Wallace But you don't use it?

Livia (*firmly*) No, not at all.

Wallace Don't you find writing a lonely occupation?

Livia No, not at all! (*Quickly changing the subject*) Why didn't you go on writing? It seems such a shame to give up once you've taken the trouble to start. After all, it takes as much effort to write a bad book as a good book. In any case plenty of bad books get published.

Wallace I don't think I wrote a bad book — not at all. I tried to get it published but failed. I felt discouraged.

Livia What was it about — your book?

Wallace Relationships.

Livia Relationships? That interests all writers. That's what life is about, isn't it, relationships, connections?

Wallace For instance — I've found it quite intriguing watching what's going on here.

Livia In what way?

Wallace Oh you and your husband meeting up with an old friend and *her* husband — it seemed to create some friction, I thought.

Livia Was that so obvious?

Wallace Oh, rather. I'm afraid your friend doesn't like you, Livia, probably never did …

Livia I can never understand it when people don't like me.

Wallace Do you care — whether people like you or not?

Livia (*after a pause*) I suppose I don't — not really.

Wallace Do you like yourself?

Livia Why yes — don't you?

Wallace Only sometimes.

Ashley enters through the archway

Ashley I thought I heard voices.

Livia Oh — Wallace and I were just talking about relationships.

Ashley A fascinating subject.

Wallace How is your wife?

Ashley She'll be all right. Didn't hurt herself at all except for a little bruise on the knee. Good job she hit the post. The way she was driving if she'd gone out on the main road she might have killed herself!

Wallace You don't think that was her intention?

Ashley Oh no — why should it be?

Wallace (*after a pause*) Just a thought! Ah well, I think I'll just go into the garden for a smoke. See you later.

Wallace exits via the french windows

Ashley I hoped I'd find you alone. (*He tries to take Livia into his arms*)

Livia (*resisting him*) I'm so thrilled! I've actually got a good idea for a plot! I've started writing again.

Ashley Oh, good — listen, darling … (*He trys again to embrace her*)

Livia (*pushing him away*) No, you listen. (*She moves across stage in front of him*) How do you like this? "They collapsed in an agony of passion into the long grass …"

Ashley (*following her*) Collapsed? But we didn't, did we? There wasn't time.

Livia (*irritably*) It isn't about us! Still, perhaps collapsed is a bit strong. What about "sank down".

Ashley (*putting his arms round her*) That's better — quite sexy.

Livia (*wriggling away*) It's meant to be.

Ashley (*disappointedly*) So that's all I am, is it, a project?

Livia You know you're not.

Ashley A project or an object of your purple prose?

Livia Neither — and I don't think it is purple prose. I'm not writing about us — seeing you again may have inspired me, but that doesn't mean it's about us — not at all!

Ashley (*peeved*) If you say so!

Livia Are you sure Patsy's all right? Why did she do such a stupid thing?

Ashley She was just hysterical. Suspecting things.

Livia About us?

Ashley Of course. What else?

Livia But what made her suspicious?

Ashley I've been trying to tell you. Someone left her a note saying we'd met before.

Livia Oh, I don't like that. That means someone *knows*. They must do.

Ashley I must say it gave me a bit of a turn.

Livia And she believed it?

Ashley Enough to make her feel like a suicidal drive. Lucky that post got in the way. She's a rotten enough driver even when she isn't having a tantrum!

Livia Have you managed to convince her it wasn't true — the note?

Ashley Lied through my teeth — but I still feel nervous about it, naturally. What about Stanley?

Livia He's all right. He thinks it's all part of the game.

Ashley The game?

Livia Yes — you know. The murder weekend.

Ashley My God! I'd forgotten all about that.

Livia That's why we're here.

Ashley Of course it is. I'd forgotten.

Livia It's horrible to think someone *knows* about us!

Ashley It could be just a guess — we have been a bit indiscreet, after all.

Livia In the garden? Yes — I suppose we have. But still to say we'd met before …

Ashley The note didn't actually say we'd met, it simply posed the question had we met? Not quite the same thing.

Livia I'm just getting paranoid — the situation is so out of hand!

They look at one another glumly

Ashley I wish we were somewhere else ... (*He leans towards her*)
Livia (*moving away*) But we're not, are we?

Dotty and Vi are heard talking offstage. Ashley moves swiftly DR. *Livia is* DL

Dotty and Vi enter through the archway

Dotty I'm so cross I missed it all. You must have had a much better view from down here ...
Vi I had — clearly. I saw them all run down to the car and then carry the woman out. She'd fainted or collapsed or something and they brought her in and straight upstairs — very dramatic! (*Suddenly aware of Ashley*) Oh, Mr McAvoy — how is your wife?
Ashley Oh — not too bad. I was just going up there actually — see if she wants anything ...

Ashley exits through the archway

Dotty He didn't look concerned. She must be all right. (*To Livia*) What do you think, darling?
Livia I think she'll be all right.
Dotty I missed all the action. I was in the bathroom at the time when she was brought in.
Livia Apparently it was just an accident. She missed her footing on the brake and hit the post at the end of the drive.
Vi She wasn't hurt?
Livia Not really! Just upset.
Dotty It couldn't be part of the plot, could it, darling?
Livia Oh, no, she wouldn't want to damage her car deliberately, would she?
Dotty She might not have meant to do any damage. She might have just been trying to make a point.
Livia A dramatic gesture that misfired? That would be like Patsy! Anyway, I don't really care. I'm not enjoying it any more.
Dotty What — the murder weekend?
Livia Yes, it's getting boring.
Vi Boring! I would hardly call it boring — a girl disappears, we don't know where or why or even how, and now Mrs McAvoy has had an accident ...
Livia The thing is I have a really good idea for a story and I want to get on with it.
Vi What an odd thing to say!
Livia I'm sorry, I didn't mean to sound so callous.

Stanley enters through the archway, beaming happily. His whole manner is more cheerful than formerly

Stanley Any new developments?

Livia I've only written two pages ...

Stanley I meant in the plot here, darling, not what you're writing.

Vi Your wife said she's bored with it.

Stanley Is she? Are you bored, darling?

Livia A bit.

Stanley But why? I thought you played your part very well — very well indeed. All that nonsense making Patsy jealous! So clever. I'm quite glad I didn't realize what was going on. I wouldn't have been able to make it anywhere near as plausible as you did!

Dotty Didn't anyone call an ambulance?

Stanley Of course not. We can't have *real* police, *real* ambulances! Whatever next?

Dotty So long as she's *really* all right.

Wallace enters via the french windows

Stanley Of course she is. She was a bit upset but I don't think it was to do with the car. *My* wife never gets upset when she hits something — does it too often, I suppose!

Livia I do get upset.

Stanley Yes, but not hysterical.

Dotty I do wish I'd been down here. It's like missing the first act of a play. I don't really know what's going on.

Vi Well — we can guess or make it up!

Dotty Of course. We can work it out between us.

Wallace I'm sorry — I only caught the tail-end of this conversation but you're surely not suggesting the accident was part of it — this whole business!

Livia Of course not! It's too absurd!

Mrs Johnson enters behind the desk

Mrs Johnson How is Mrs McAvoy? I really think we should have had a doctor.

Stanley crosses to her with a jocular expression

Stanley Have you got a nephew who's a doctor?

Mrs Johnson What do you mean?

Stanley Like the policeman who's a nephew, eh?

Mrs Johnson That's different. Quite different.

Stanley Is it?

Ashley rushes in through the archway

Ashley Call an ambulance — somebody quick!
Stanley What now?
Ashley My wife! She just stood there in the bathroom throwing pills down her throat — a mouthful at a time! I don't know what they were, sleeping pills, I suppose! We must *do* something. She wouldn't let me help — she fought me off and shoved me out of the bathroom and locked the door. Please help me!
Stanley We'll break the door down!

Stanley and Ashley start to move towards the archway

Mrs Johnson (*quickly coming round from behind desk*) No, please don't! There's a ladder by the back wall. You can reach the bathroom window easily.
Stanley Good thinking, Mrs Johnson! Come on, let's get it!
Mrs Johnson (*moving towards Stanley and Ashley*) You don't have to break the window. It doesn't close properly.
Stanley Don't worry, we won't break anything. Show me the way!

Mrs Johnson and Stanley exit through the archway

Ashley is about to follow when Livia takes hold of his arm

Livia Ashley — what *is* happening?
Ashley I just don't know …

They exit in a hurry through the archway

Pause. Dotty and Vi exchange glances

Wallace Well — ladies — can you work it out?

CURTAIN

SCENE 3

The same. Later that night

The curtains are drawn at the french windows. The standard lamp is turned on

As the CURTAIN *rises, Livia is curled up in the armchair* DR *writing vigorously in a notebook*

During the following, Mrs Johnson enters quietly and stands behind the desk listening

Livia, unaware of Mrs Johnson, stops writing

Livia (*reading from the notebook*) "... as they surrendered to their mutual passion, flesh on pulsating flesh, throbbing heart on heart, she threw away the last vestige of respectable veneer. If this was to be their last night together she vowed it would be their best, a night of passion to end all others and to live forever in her memory ..."

Livia looks up

Mrs Johnson Excuse me — I don't know what to do about dinner. Are they still at the hospital?
Livia Ashley and my husband? Yes, as far as I know. I don't know how Patsy is. My husband insisted on following the ambulance in his car to bring Ashley back. Ashley was in such a state, you see — went to pieces. I was quite surprised.
Mrs Johnson You didn't want to go?
Livia Oh, no. There didn't seem much point in a deputation going, did there? I'm sure she'll be all right. You see, I know Patsy of old. She just has an hysterical personality. Attention-seeking, that's all she was doing. She knew very well she'd recover and be sorted out, otherwise she wouldn't have stood there in front of Ashley and done it, would she? Anyone who really wants to commit suicide does it secretly on their own, not with a great dramatic gesture in front of someone.
Mrs Johnson It's all very upsetting.
Livia Yes, it has been. But there's nothing we can do about it, is there? (*She returns to her writing*)
Mrs Johnson The whole weekend has been ruined really. Mrs Padmore and Mrs Jenkins have gone off to Rye. They don't seem to be a bit interested in what's going on here. Nothing's going according to plan. I won't want to do another murder weekend in a hurry, I can tell you.

Livia (*still preoccupied*) I shouldn't!
Mrs Johnson Oh — has it been that bad? I am sorry! I have tried.

Livia does not respond

(*Adding forcibly*) I said I have tried.
Livia Oh, sorry! I wasn't really paying attention. You see, I've just had a
splendid idea for a story and I must get it down on paper before I forget it.
Lately I've had writer's block. I just couldn't write at all but suddenly I
seem to have come unblocked and I must write it down while it's fresh in
my head.
Mrs Johnson I am sorry to bother you — I'll leave you alone.
Livia I didn't mean to be rude. Actually, I think I'll be all right now I've got
going again. It's such a relief.
Mrs Johnson This weekend has achieved something then.
Livia Oh yes — quite a lot! I'm really grateful.
Mrs Johnson I'm glad somebody is ... (*She turns to go*)
Livia Oh, Mrs Johnson ...
Mrs Johnson Yes?
Livia My husband is quite of the opinion that everything that has happened
so far has been part of the plot, at least up until Patsy's display of histrionics!
Mrs Johnson Everything? Oh, I don't think I can claim *everything*. I'm not
quite that inventive.
Livia That's what I thought. I don't mean you're not inventive, but I do
happen to know *everything* hasn't been part of the plot because I know the
bits I'm in are not part of the plot! However, I don't mind if that's what he
wants to think.
Mrs Johnson I see. (*Though clearly she doesn't*)

*The telephone rings. Livia returns to her writing while Mrs Johnson answers
the phone*

Mrs Johnson (*into the phone*) Crossways Hotel. May I help you? ... Who?
... I'm sorry I don't know what you mean. ...(*With surprise*) Are you sure?
... Yes, of course I'll come right away. (*She hangs up*)
Livia (*with only mild curiosity*) Anything wrong?
Mrs Johnson (*puzzled*) I'm not sure. But I have to go somewhere. Will you
be all right? There are no staff on duty at present.
Livia Of course I'll be all right. I don't mind being alone a bit. I can get on
with my new story.
Mrs Johnson Oh, good! I don't suppose I'll be long.

Mrs Johnson goes off quickly

Livia returns to her writing

Livia Now then — a row of dots and then ... (*Reading from her notebook*) "He left the warmth of her bed as she still slumbered. He showered, relinquishing for the last time the scent of her body." No." ... the scent of her *dear* body clinging to his flesh as he tried to dismiss the haunting memory of that last desperate embrace. He knew this parting must be their last one — he wondered how he could bear to go on without her but he knew he must." (*She gives a little sigh of satisfaction and sits back to think*)

The curtains at the french windows stir slightly. Livia looks at them thoughtfully and then looks down at the floor

A pair of feet (Wallace's feet) can be seen underneath the curtain

Livia notices

Darling — don't hide behind the curtain. I'm quite alone! (*She rises and pulls back the curtain*)

Wallace is standing there

Livia steps back with a gasp

Wallace Sorry to startle you!
Livia You did — rather! I thought you were someone else!
Wallace Obviously!
Livia I thought you were out ... I thought everyone was out.
Wallace I was out but I came back. Everyone else *is* out. I take it there's no news from the hospital?
Livia About Patsy? No — but I expect she'll be all right. They'll just pump her stomach out and send her home. I wouldn't be at all surprised if she hasn't done it before. It's pure hysteria.
Wallace You know about such things.
Livia In theory a writer has to know everything.
Wallace Knows all, feels nothing?
Livia You mean I should feel sorry for Patsy ... Well, I don't! I know her too well. I shall probably write about it some time. Haven't you heard that a writer has a heart of ice?
Wallace You don't feel guilty?
Livia Guilty? Why should I? She has a little *contretemps* with her husband and decides to take an overdose. It's nothing to do with me.
Wallace I thought — it might have been, something to do with you.

Livia Not at all! But in a way I'm grateful to her. This weekend has unblocked my creative ability. I've started writing again — after months of not being able to. Now I don't want to stop.

Wallace Don't let me stop you. I know what it's like when you're in full flow.

Livia Oh yes, you would know. I forgot you're a writer yourself.

Wallace No, not a writer, merely a failed writer.

Livia I understand. (*She sits down again in an armchair* DR) I felt like that for a while. But I've got it back at last. I've practically written a short story this afternoon. In fact it's so good it might even become the first chapter of a novel — one in the great British romantic tradition. I can hardly wait to get home and transfer it all to my computer.

Wallace That's the way you write, is it? On your computer?

Livia Of course. It's an absolute boon — so easy to correct as you go along. Just imagine what it was like tapping everything out on an old manual! Or even worse writing by long-hand? All those novels by Dickens, what an effort!

Wallace You're a whiz on the Internet, as well, I take it.

Livia I've taught myself. It's so useful, isn't it? For research and so on …

Wallace There's a website, isn't there? "Writers United" . For lonely writers to make contact with one another and exchange ideas. That was what it's for, isn't it? The exchange of ideas?

Livia (*warily*) You mentioned that before — the chat line. You're not a private detective are you?

Wallace (*amused*) Why should you think that? Is there anything to detect?

Livia No, of course not. It was just — your interest.

Wallace My interest?

Livia In the same things that interest me.

Wallace (*airily*) Coincidence, don't you think? I love coincidence in writing, don't you? A handy little tool to move the plot on.

Livia becomes disturbed by the turn of the conversation. She shuts her notebook and rises

Livia Yes, it may be, but I don't really believe in coincidence, you see. Not in real life.

Wallace That surprises me.

Livia (*frostily*) Why should it surprise you? You hardly know me. How can anything about me surprise you! (*She looks as if she is going to leave through the archway*)

Wallace blocks her way

Wallace Don't go! I want to talk to you.

Livia I'm not sure I want to talk to you.

Wallace Oh, I think you will do when you hear what I have to say.

Livia (*crossly*) Doesn't it occur to you I might not be interested?

Wallace Ah, but you will be! Think about it. We are quite alone. Your husband and your friend's husband are at the hospital fifteen miles away. The two ladies accepted my suggestion to go into Rye for the afternoon. Mrs Johnson has gone off on a wild goose chase after my phone call that they'd found Shelley. It will take her at least an hour to discover that was a hoax. In the meantime we are quite alone — and you are going to listen to me!

Livia (*intrigued despite her alarm*) *Your* phone call? About Shelley? Do you know where she is then? I don't understand. What are you playing at?

Wallace I'm about to tell you — if you'll listen!

Wallace pushes her into the chair above the table DL

Livia Why should I?

Wallace Curiosity, my dear Livia! The curiosity of a writer. You see, I know all about you and your little liaison with Ashley McAvoy — I've known about it from the start and followed it with interest.

Livia (*stiffly*) I don't know what you mean.

Wallace Don't waste time, Livia. You used to meet at the *Red Cow* in Great Stoughton. I know because I was there the first time you met and after that I monitored your meetings. I even know which motel you used for your romantic matinées.

Livia I don't understand. Was it you who left that note for Patsy then? But why? Why make such mischief? What point was there in it?

Wallace Yes, I left the note. I wanted to see what would happen. It's fun sometimes to manipulate people — you must know that yourself. I wanted to see what real people would do instead of fictional characters. Just a little research for something I'm working on.

Livia But she might have died.

Wallace That was the chance I took.

Livia The chance *you* took. What about *her*?

Wallace I thought you didn't care about her. Just now you were dismissing her suicide bid as a dramatic gesture.

Livia (*rising indignantly*) That doesn't mean I don't *care* about her. She's an old friend.

Wallace I must admit that was one thing that threw me — the fact that you two knew one another. However, I found a way to use it to my advantage.

Livia *Your* advantage? You're not making sense.

Wallace Did you ever tell the inimitable Ashley that you had met someone else on the Internet — before him?

Livia No — because I didn't meet anyone else.

Wallace No, you didn't actually meet anyone else. But you *arranged* to meet someone else.

Livia How do you know?

Wallace I know because the person you arranged to meet was me.

Livia (*scornfully*) You! Don't be absurd. (*She crosses in front of him* DR) It wasn't you. It couldn't have been.

Wallace You admit it then — you did arrange to meet someone?

Livia I did arrange a perfectly harmless little meeting about a couple of months before I met Ashley, but the person didn't turn up.

Wallace The person did turn up. I turned up and sat observing you. You had supplied me with a photograph, remember — but I hadn't reciprocated. I told you I'd approach you, but of course I didn't. I *observed*. It was in the *Red Cow*, the very place where you later met Ashley. You gave it half an hour waiting for someone to turn up and then left. I followed you home. So then I had all the information I needed. I knew how to contact you and I knew where you lived.

Livia I don't understand. What was the point of all that? If you wanted to meet me why didn't you do so in a straightforward manner? Why the secrecy? It seems so silly!

Wallace Silly to you perhaps! But I enjoyed sitting looking at you, knowing you were waiting for someone — for me — and that I could or could not come forward as I chose. I enjoyed the feeling of power that gave me. I thought my not turning up would arouse your curiosity, your interest. I wanted that most of all, to arouse your interest. I intended to make another arrangement to meet you, and this time I would be there armed with so much more knowledge about you than you had about me. That was important to me.

Livia I didn't encourage you to have such ideas about me. You knew I was married.

Wallace Well — yes, but I also knew you were looking for romance. That was clear from your writing and from our electronic conversations. You were desperate for something to happen in your life, something exciting.

Livia That's not true! I'm sorry if I gave you that impression. If you are the man I wrote to and I suppose you are because you know so much about me, I thought of you simply as a friend, a fellow writer. I must admit I couldn't understand why you didn't turn up for that meeting but after that I just didn't bother with you any more.

Wallace Yes, it was unexpected the way you ceased writing to me. You didn't even open my emails. A touch arrogant I thought. But I didn't give up on you. I was determined to meet you. I dogged you, to be frank, waiting for the right moment, the right time.

Livia (*horrified*) You were stalking me!

Wallace (*with modest pride*) I suppose I was. Unfortunately, before I could make contact again you met Ashley McAvoy, and found the romance you were looking for. That upset me.

Livia (*after a pause*) I don't believe all this. You're just trying to frighten me. It's all part of the plot, isn't it? The murder weekend? The others will come back in a minute and we'll have a laugh about it.

Wallace Oh no, my dear. Nobody will have a laugh — least of all you!

Livia But how did you know about this weekend? Why are you here? It doesn't make sense.

Wallace It was all planned, my dear, I assure you. I arranged it all, it gave me a great sense of power. You were my puppets!

Livia This is ridiculous! My mother-in-law booked this weekend. There was a card accompanying the letter. "Happy Anniversary. Mother."

Wallace Did you check with her?

Livia I couldn't. She's on a cruise — I never thought of it. I knew it must be her.

Wallace You knew wrong, my dear. I made sure your mother-in-law was away. *I* sent the booking. I also sent the booking to your lover. Not a man of great principal, is he, Mr Ashley? He didn't check up in case it was a mistake. It was *free* after all.

Livia I don't believe you did all this. How was it possible?

Wallace I had access to your emails, my dear, that's how. What a lot that tells one, better than bugging the phone and much easier! Don't look so surprised. It isn't difficult.

Livia You had no right to snoop into my private life!

Wallace Then perhaps you should have been more careful who you met on the Internet, my dear. You were prepared to arouse the interest of men even though you weren't free. Didn't you realize what you might uncover, what passion you might arouse? Look at me! I have become obsessed with you. I can't rest, I can't sleep, I can't write, I can't think about anything else but you. You haunt me!

Livia (*after a pause*) I think you're in urgent need of help!

Wallace I did need help, I needed your help, but I think it's too late, now. My plan misfired. Seeing Ashley with his wife I thought you would realize how worthless he was, instead of which you fell into his arms! It sickened me! I decided then that if I couldn't have you no-one else would.

Livia What do you mean by that?

Wallace I came prepared. (*He produces a revolver from his pocket*)

Livia You're bluffing. (*She backs away from him*)

Wallace I'm afraid not. (*He pushes her into the armchair* DR)

Livia (*nervously*) You surely don't mean to kill me? You won't get away with it — you're being very foolish. There's DNA and ... And finger prints and everything.

Wallace To match me with my DNA they have to find me first. I don't exist as far as this hotel is concerned. And I shall be rid of a terrible obsession.

Wallace takes hold of Livia's throat and then circles the chair until he is behind her

Livia Please don't!
Wallace I'm sorry, my dear, but there is no way out.

Wallace holds Livia's head and puts the barrel of the gun in her neck from behind

Livia (*struggling*) No, please …

Shelley enters hurriedly through the archway

Shelley I'm looking for Mrs Johnson. Oh, who are you? What are you doing?

Wallace puts his hand across Livia's mouth, concealing the gun behind her back. Livia struggles and gasps

Wallace We're just rehearsing for tonight — for the denouement. (*To Livia*) Do calm down, dear — (*with menace*) you wouldn't like anyone *else* to get hurt, would you?
Shelley Isn't it over yet? I thought someone would have worked it out by now, and then my dad told me a lady had gone to hospital and I thought it must be over, so I came back. I was fed up at home. Where's Mrs Johnson?
Wallace Oh, she's somewhere around. It was her idea we should rehearse. Spice it up a bit for when the others come back. It had all gone a bit tame — for a murder weekend.
Shelley Well, that's not my fault. You were all supposed to work out what had happened to me, instead of that you've all been having a jolly time. I thought you were all a bit thick, actually.
Wallace Some of us became — distracted. Tell you what, Shelley, if you're back on duty a cup of tea wouldn't come amiss.
Shelley Yes, all right. (*With a puzzled look at Livia*) You are taking your rehearsing a bit far, aren't you? The poor lady looks as if she can hardly breathe.
Wallace We thought we'd make it realistic. It's a red herring really …
Shelley It don't look much like a red herring. It's only a game, isn't it?
Wallace Of course it is. Now what about that cup of tea, Shelley …
Shelley Yes, all right. (*She turns to go*)

Livia struggles violently and pulls Wallace's hand away from her mouth

Livia (*gasping*) Don't go!
Shelley (*turning round*) What?

Wallace has Livia under control once more

Wallace Mrs Wagstaff would like some biscuits.
Shelley All right. I was going to bring some biscuits anyway.

Shelley goes out

Wallace Sorry, my dear, but you won't escape that easily! We'll go outside
and do it. I don't want the girl alarmed. It would be a pity to kill her too!
Livia You wouldn't!
Wallace If I had to. Now just get outside.

Wallace forces Livia across to the french windows

Over there behind the trees where you used to meet Ashley, a perfect spot
for a murder!

Shelley enters

Shelley Mrs Johnson locks everything up in the kitchen when she's out so
I can't make tea.

Livia digs her elbow into Wallace's ribs and moves away from him

Livia Look out, Shelley! He has a gun!

Shelley lets out a scream

Shelley Oh, Daddy! Save me!

Wallace levels his gun and fires

*Livia dives to the floor. Shelley lets out a loud scream and collapses. A door
slams off stage*

Mrs Johnson (*off stage*) What was that?

*Wallace looks round desperately and exits via the french windows. Mrs
Johnson enters and stares at the two women*

Livia slowly rises and looks round cautiously

Livia Has he gone?
Mrs Johnson Who?
Livia Mr Wainwright. He had a gun.
Mrs Johnson Good heavens! What on earth was he doing with it!
Livia Shooting it!

Shelley groans

Livia He shot Shelley!
Mrs Johnson Shot Shelley! How awful!

Both women lean over Shelley who groans again

Shelley (*sitting up*) What happened?
Livia Are you hurt?
Mrs Johnson You poor dear! That nasty Mr Wainwright shot you.

Shelley screams and faints

Mrs Johnson Oh dear — she must be hurt.
Livia I can't see any blood.
Mrs Johnson (*resentfully*) You don't always see blood — in films.
Livia You don't see blood in old black and white movies, you do in modern films. When someone is shot there's blood everywhere!
Mrs Johnson I am glad I didn't have the new carpet laid. I'm keeping it for the spring.

Shelley groans again and sits up

Shelley Where am I?
Livia How do you feel?
Shelley I don't know.
Mrs Johnson (*tentatively*) Any pain anywhere, dear?
Shelley (*groaning*) My head! (*She rubs the back of her head*)
Livia I don't see any blood.
Shelley Why should there be blood?
Mrs Johnson We thought you were shot.

Shelley is about to scream

Livia Don't faint! I thought he'd missed me and hit you, but now I think he missed both of us! Rotten shot!
Shelley Oh yes — I remember now — that man ...(*She is about to scream*)
Livia It's all right. He's gone!

Livia and Mrs Johnson help Shelley to an armchair DR

You'll never know how fortunate it was, Mrs Johnson, that you came back when you did!
Mrs Johnson I was sent on a wild goose-chase looking for Shelley, by some anonymous caller, but of course she wasn't where he said she was and then I ran into my nephew who brought me back.
Shelley (*dazed*) That awful man! Why would he want to shoot me?
Livia He didn't want to shoot you. He wanted to shoot me.
Mrs Johnson Shoot you?
Livia I thought it was part of the game.
Mrs Johnson If it was he should have told me. He didn't have a part to play, he came too late.

The front doorbell rings

Mrs Johnson Who can that be? Excuse me!

Mrs Johnson exits through the archway

Shelley (*sniffing and sobbing*) It *was* part of the game, wasn't it? It was silly of me to faint.
Livia (*reassuringly*) Yes, it must have been part of the game.
Shelley He did frighten me. It was so realistic. I really thought I'd been shot.
Livia He must have been firing blanks.
Shelley I wish I'd never agreed to take part. I only did it to help Mrs Johnson out. She was so keen to make it a really unusual weekend that you would all remember for ever!
Livia She succeeded there!

Mrs Johnson enters looking pleased

Mrs Johnson What a stroke of luck! That was my nephew. He'd just dropped me off when Wainwright ran round the side of the hotel waving a gun in the air. He's been arrested, of course.
Shelley What for?
Mrs Johnson Well — you can't go round with a loaded fire-arm, can you? Not in England!
Shelley Loaded! With real bullets!
Mrs Johnson I assume so!

Shelley promptly faints again. Mrs Johnson fusses over Shelley

Stanley enters via the french windows

Stanley What is going on?

Livia (*running to him*) Stanley — thank God, you're back!

Stanley What has been happening? There's a police car at the door with Wainwright sitting in the back. He looks pretty grim.

Livia So he should.

Stanley What's wrong with *her*?

Mrs Johnson She'll be all right. I'll just take her into the kitchen and we'll make a cup of tea. Come along now, Shelley. Pull yourself together, dear.

Shelley groans and picks herself up

Shelley I'm sorry. I was scared. Oh, dear that awful man ...

Mrs Johnson There, there, you'll be all right now, dear. Don't worry about it — he's gone now.

Shelley and Mrs Johnson go off through the archway

Stanley Good heavens, that was Shelley! The one who disappeared.

Livia She came back.

Stanley What was she talking about? I don't understand. What are the police doing with Wainwright? It's surely not part of the murder weekend.

Livia No, no, of course not. They've arrested him and I hope they keep him under lock and key.

Stanley But what has he done?

Livia I'll explain — I'll try to explain, but it might be difficult. You might hear things about me that you won't like, darling, but you won't believe them, will you?

Stanley What sort of things?

Livia Oh, adverse things. Untrue things! You won't believe them, will you, darling.

Stanley After this weekend I'll never hear another word against you, darling. I'm not making a fool of myself again!

Livia Oh, darling, I knew you'd take it like that. (*Giving him a hug*) I'm so pleased you came back. You've no idea!

Stanley (*surprised*) I don't suppose I've been gone more than a couple of hours!

Livia But so much has happened! I do appreciate you.

Stanley (*delighted*) That's good! I must go away more often! What shall we do now?

Livia Let's go home.

Stanley Suits me! Don't you want to know about Patsy?

Livia Oh, I'd forgotten. How is she?

Stanley She's all right. They pumped her stomach out and she's sitting up as if nothing had happened. I left Ashley with her. He's all over the silly woman, so I suppose she's got what she wanted, brought him in line.

Livia (*disappointed*) He's really making a fuss of her?

Stanley He certainly is! I suppose he realized he didn't want to lose her when he thought he had.

Pause

Livia Let's go home, Stanley. I really want to.

Stanley Suits me! I can't say I've enjoyed the weekend much.

Livia Nor have I, except it started me writing again.

Stanley Yes, that's good!

Livia I've got a really good idea for a short story — in fact it might even make a full-length novel.

Stanley Jolly good! Come upstairs and tell me about it, while we pack ...

Stanley puts his arm around Livia affectionately

Livia You see, this couple turn up for a murder weekend in a country hotel ...

They move towards the archway as if to exit

The CURTAIN *falls*

FURNITURE AND PROPERTY LIST

ACT I

SCENE 1

On stage: Desk/counter. *On it*: bell, telephone, registration book and pen. *Above it*: board with hotel keys
Two chairs
Small table DL
Two armchairs
Occasional table DR
Standard lamp
Curtains open at french windows

Off stage: Suitcase (**Stanley**)
Vanity case (**Livia**)
Tray with tea for two (**Shelley**)
Report (**Stanley**)
Suitcase (**Vi**)
Suitcase (**Dotty**)

Personal: **Ashley**: cigarettes

SCENE 2

Strike: Tea tray and contents from small table DL
Livia's vanity case

Personal: **Patsy**: white envelope

ACT II

SCENE 1

Set: Newspaper on small table DL

Off stage: Two cups of tea on a tray
Suitcase (**Livia**)

Personal: **Patsy**: folded slip of paper

SCENE 2

Strike: Two cups and saucers from DL and DR, newspaper, suitcase

Set: Notebook and pencil for **Livia**

SCENE 3

Re-set: Curtains closed at french windows

Personal: **Wallace**: revolver

MANAGEMENT OF FIREARMS AND OTHER WEAPONS IN PRODUCTIONS

Recommended reading:

Entertainment Information Sheet No. 20 (Health and Safety Executive). This information sheet is one of a series produced in consultation with the Joint Advisory Committee for Broadcasting and the Performing Arts. It gives guidance on the management of weapons that are part of a production, including firearms, replicas and deactivated weapons. It is obtainable from: HSE Books, PO Box 1999, Sudbury, Suffolk, CO10 2WA. Tel: 01787 881165, Fax: 01787 313995. Or it may be downloaded from: www.hse.gov.uk

Home Office Firearms Law: Guidance to the Police. The Stationery Office 2002. ISBN 0 11 341273 8. Also available from: www.homeoffice.gov.uk

Health and Safety in Audio-visual Production: Your legal duties. Leaflet INDG360. HSE Books 2002

LIGHTING PLOT

Practical fittings required: standard lamp
1 interior with exterior backing behind french windows. Same throughout

ACT I, SCENE 1. Afternoon

To open: Daytime interior with afternoon exterior

Cue 1   **Ashley**: " Oh my God! Sherlock Holmes!"   (Page 18)
                Black-out

ACT I, SCENE 2. Morning

To open: Daytime interior with morning exterior

No cues

ACT II, SCENE 1. Afternoon

To open: Daytime interior with afternoon exterior

No cues

ACT II, SCENE 2. Evening

To open: Evening interior with evening exterior

No cues

ACT II, SCENE 3. Night

To open: General interior with practical and covering spot; night exterior

No cues

EFFECTS PLOT

ACT I

ACT II